THE PSYCHOLOGY OF SPENDING

Unraveling the mysteries behind
our financial choices

JONAS CHARLES KPABITEY

Copyright © 2024 Copyright © 2024 by Jonas Charles Kpabitey
All rights reserved.

No part of this publication may be reproduced, distributed, or transmitted in any form or by any means, including photocopying, recording, or other electronic or mechanical methods, without the prior written permission of the copyright owner, except in the case of brief quotations embodied in critical reviews and certain other noncommercial uses permitted by copyright law.

The book is dedicated to God all mighty and everyone who participated to make this book a masterpiece to read.

CONTENTS

Title Page
Copyright
Dedication
Introduction
Preface

Chapter 1	1
Chapter 2	5
Chapter 3	8
Chapter 4	11
Chapter 5	15
Chapter 6	17
CONCLUSION	20
Acknowledgement	21
Books By This Author	23

INTRODUCTION

Welcome to the captivating world of the psychology of spending, where our desires, emotions, and societal influences intertwine to shape our financial behaviors. In this modern era of consumerism, it is essential to understand the underlying factors that drive our spending habits and the impact they have on our overall well-being.

Have you ever found yourself impulsively purchasing items you didn't truly need, only to experience a fleeting sense of satisfaction followed by regret? Or perhaps you have fallen victim to the allure of sales and discounts, succumbing to the pressure of limited-time offers. If so, you are not alone. Millions of individuals around the world grapple with the complexities of spending and its profound psychological effects.

"The Mindful Spender: Unraveling the Psychology of Spending and Cultivating Healthy Financial Habits" is a journey into the depths of our consumer-driven society, aiming to shed light on the intricate workings of our minds and emotions when it comes to spending. Through understanding the psychological forces at play, we can gain insight into our spending behaviors and develop strategies to make more conscious and intentional financial decisions.

This book explores the multifaceted aspects of consumer behavior, delving into the pleasure of acquisition, the influence of social comparison, the role of emotions, the power of advertising, and the fear of missing out (FOMO). We will examine the neurological basis of our desire for possessions, the impact of social pressures on our spending choices, and how emotions can lead to impulsive buying and retail therapy.

By unraveling the psychology behind our spending habits, we can begin to reclaim control over our financial lives. This book will guide you on a transformative journey towards mindful spending, where you align your purchases with your personal values, priorities, and long-term goals. Through mindful spending, you can break free from the cycle of mindless consumption and cultivate a more fulfilling and purpose-driven financial life.

"The Mindful Spender" provides practical strategies, thought-provoking insights, and actionable steps to help you navigate the complex landscape of spending. It encourages you to cultivate a deeper self-awareness, challenge societal pressures, and make conscious choices that align with your true desires and aspirations.

This book is not about depriving yourself of the joys of life, but rather, it is about empowering yourself to make informed decisions and live a life of financial freedom and contentment. By understanding the psychology of spending, you can embark on a path of personal growth, nurturing a positive relationship with money and creating a brighter future for yourself.

Now, let us embark on this enlightening journey into the psychology of spending, as we unravel the intricacies of our consumer-driven world and discover the transformative power of mindful financial habits.

PREFACE

In a world filled with enticing advertisements, endless product options, and the constant pressure to keep up with the latest trends, it's no wonder that many of us find ourselves caught in the grip of impulsive and mindless spending. The psychology of spending is a fascinating and complex subject that delves into the intricate workings of our minds, emotions, and societal influences.

"The Mindful Spender: Unraveling the Psychology of Spending and Cultivating Healthy Financial Habits" aims to shed light on the underlying factors that drive our spending behaviors and empower readers to develop a more mindful and intentional approach to their financial decisions. By exploring the captivating world of consumer behavior and the impact of emotions, social pressures, and advertising, this book offers valuable insights into the psychology of spending.

In today's consumer-driven society, it is all too easy to fall into the trap of impulsive buying, seeking temporary emotional fulfillment through retail therapy, and succumbing to the fear of missing out (FOMO). However, through a deeper understanding of the psychological forces at play, we can break free from the cycle of mindless spending and embark on a journey toward financial well-being and contentment.

"The Mindful Spender" is not just a guide to curbing spending habits; it also explores the concept of mindful spending, where individuals cultivate a deeper awareness of their values, priorities, and long-term goals. By aligning spending choices with personal values, individuals can create a more fulfilling and purpose-driven financial life, free from the burden of unnecessary purchases and debt.

This book is not about deprivation or denying oneself the joys of life; instead, it invites readers to embark on a transformative journey of self-discovery. By recognizing the psychological factors that drive our spending habits, we can develop strategies to overcome impulsive urges, resist the allure of sales and discounts, and make conscious financial decisions that align with our true desires and aspirations.

"The Mindful Spender" offers practical tools, thought-provoking insights, and actionable steps to help readers transform their spending habits and cultivate healthy financial practices. I hope that this book will serve as a guiding light, illuminating the path toward financial freedom, mindful consumption, and a more fulfilling relationship with money.

Remember, your financial well-being is within your control. By understanding the psychology of spending and adopting a mindful approach, you have the power to shape your financial destiny and create a life of abundance and contentment.

Let us embark on this eye-opening journey into the psychology of spending, as we unravel the intricacies of our consumer-driven world and discover the true meaning of financial freedom and fulfillment.

CHAPTER 1

Mindful Spending: Aligning Your Purchases with Your Values

Have we asked ourselves these questions? ***What if we could change our approach to spending?***

What if we could adopt a more mindful and intentional mindset when it comes to our purchases? Does it sound rhetorical? We will explore the concept of mindful spending and how it can transform our relationship with money and bring us closer to living a life aligned with our values as far as our financial life is concerned.

What if we could change our approach to spending?

To develop a more satisfying and meaningful connection with money, we need to change the way we spend it. Aligning our purchases with our values and desires can help us discover fulfillment and escape the cycle of consumerism by taking a conscious approach. In addition to accepting delayed gratification and educating ourselves on the full costs and effects of our purchases, we should place a higher value on experiences than tangible belongings. Because of this, there will be a demand for goods and services that put social and environmental responsibility first, resulting in a more aware and accountable economy. Living a more purposeful and happy life and finding happiness in matching our purchases to our ideals is possible when we adopt mindful spending.

What if we could adopt a more mindful and intentional mindset

when it comes to our purchases?

Our relationship with money and consumerism can be profoundly altered by embracing an intentional and attentive mindset. By concentrating on our goals and reasons, we can cut back on unnecessary expenses and direct funds towards satisfying activities. This kind of thinking disproves popular myths about materialism by acknowledging that real fulfillment originates from following one's passions and personal development. We are no longer driven to follow fashions or partake in mindless consumerism.

Developing a mindful mentality motivates us to look for goods and services that are socially conscious, sustainably sourced, and ethically made. We help create a more conscientious economy by endorsing businesses that share our beliefs. Furthermore, making conscious and aware purchases results in a more sustainable use of resources, which lowers waste and excess. By reducing consumption and supporting long-lasting items, this change helps the environment and our pocketbooks. In the end, having an intentional and attentive mindset gives us the ability to take charge of our financial situation and live morally. By doing this, we will liberate ourselves from consumerism and make decisions that are consistent with our goals, beliefs, and the kind of world we wish to see.

Spending without thinking is a common occurrence in a world where there are a plethora of options and commercials competing for our time. Frequently, after purchasing something carelessly, we come to find out that it doesn't genuinely reflect our ideals or provide us with long-term enjoyment.

Knowing and understanding our basic beliefs is necessary to practice mindful spending. Our decisions and priorities are shaped by these values, which act as guiding principles. We may make sure that our spending represents what matters to us by ensuring that our purchases are in line with our beliefs.

If environmental sustainability, for instance, is one of our guiding principles, we can decide to promote environmentally conscious businesses or make investments in eco-friendly goods. If we value personal development and well-being, we might spend money on technologies that aid in personal growth or devote our resources to events that encourage self-improvement.

Practical Steps for Mindful Spending

1. Reflect on Your Values: Take the time to identify and reflect on your core values. What matters most to you? What do you want to prioritize in your life? Understanding your values will provide a foundation for making mindful spending decisions.

2. Research and Educate Yourself: Take the time to research the products or services you're considering. Understand the impact they have on the environment, the ethics of the companies behind them, and how well they align with your values of spending.

3. Practice Delayed Gratification: Before making a purchase, give yourself time to think it over. Delaying gratification allows you to assess whether the item aligns with your values and whether it's a wise investment of your resources.

4. Set Clear Goals: Define your financial goals and aspirations. Whether it's saving for a dream vacation, paying off debt, or investing in your education, having clear goals will help you make intentional purchasing choices that support your long-term objectives.

Mindful spending is a potent tool that can transform our relationship with money and consumption. By aligning our purchases with our values, we can make more intentional and fulfilling choices that contribute to our overall well-being and satisfaction.

Unlike impulsive or compulsive buying, mindful spending

encourages us to consider the impact of our purchases on ourselves, others, and the environment. It prompts us to question whether the item we desire is truly necessary or if there are alternative ways to fulfill that need.

CHAPTER 2

Investing for the Future: Setting Financial Goals

In the journey towards financial success, setting clear and achievable goals is crucial. Without a roadmap, it's easy to lose focus and make haphazard financial decisions.

The practice of establishing financial objectives and constructing a smart investing strategy. You'll have more direction and be better able to make decisions that support your goals if you have a clear understanding of where you want to go with your career.

What are your financial objectives?

The first step in setting financial goals is to define your objectives. Ask yourself: What do you want to achieve with your investments?

Are you saving for retirement, a new home, or your child's education?

When saving for retirement, you need to meticulously have a clear and comprehensive vision for it; Saving for retirement is an essential aspect of financial planning.

Here are some key points to consider:

As the saying goes *"The early bird catches the worms"* You need to commence early

1. *Get started early*: Your investments will have more time to grow the earlier you start saving for retirement. Over time, even modest payments can build up to a sizeable retirement account.

2. Contribute regularly: Make consistent contributions to your retirement accounts. Ideally, aim to save a percentage of your income each month. Take advantage of any employer matching contributions, as it's essentially free money.

3. Review and tweak from time to time: Make sure your retirement savings strategy is still in line with your evolving goals and financial situation by reviewing it regularly. As needed, make adjustments to your investing strategy and contributions.

4. Diversify your investments: Distribute your retirement funds over a range of securities, including equities, bonds, mutual funds, and real estate. Diversification can potentially boost profits while lowering risk.

5. Figure out what you'll need for retirement by taking stock of your income, outgoings, and savings as well as your present financial status. Estimate how much you should try to save for retirement by using internet calculators or talking to a financial counselor.

6. Choose retirement accounts: Explore different retirement accounts available in your country, such as employer-sponsored plans (e.g., 401(k) in the U.S.), individual retirement accounts (IRAs), or pensions. Each option has its own tax advantages and contribution limits.

Are you saving for a new home?

A financial aspiration that many people and families pursue is saving for a new home. To save for a new house, you need to practice financial discipline, budgeting, and careful planning—whether you're a first-time buyer or hoping to move up to a larger property.

The processes in this process include budgeting, establishing a savings target, and putting money aside for a down payment, closing charges, and other related expenses. Your dream of owning a new house can be steadily realized by creating a special savings account, automating savings payments, paying off debt, and looking into possible help programs. Making sure your savings plan fits your desired timetable and financial capabilities requires keeping an eye on property market movements and consulting with experts.

Are you saving for your child's education?

A prudent and proactive financial move, saving for your child's education can assist them have access to a top-notch school and a better future.

Preparing ahead of time and putting money aside might assist lessen the financial load when your child attends college or another higher education institution since the cost of education keeps going up. You can gradually accumulate the required amounts by beginning early and following a well-organized savings plan.

This entails deciding on your savings target, investigating the cost of education, looking into various savings methods like education savings accounts or 529 plans, and consistently making contributions to your child's education fund.

Take advantage of any potential tax benefits, think about investing methods, and make any necessary adjustments to your savings plan. Aside from offering financial assistance, saving for your child's education shows that you value their future achievement. You can make sure that your child has the financial means to follow their academic goals by making sure they have a plan and contributing consistently.

CHAPTER 3

Setting Financial SMART Goals: Specific, Measurable, Achievable, Relevant, and Time-Bound

Setting goals that are both motivating and attainable is crucial when pursuing financial success. A structure known as SMART goals guarantees that your goals are time-bound, relevant, measurable, and explicit. We'll go over each SMART goal component in this chapter and how they can help you move closer to your financial goals.

1. Specific Goals: Clarity is key

Specificity is key when establishing financial goals. Ill-defined objectives such as "save money" or "invest more" are hard to monitor and lack focus. Rather, define your goals precisely. As an example, "Save $10,000 for a down payment on a home" rather than "Invest 10% of my monthly income in a diversified portfolio." Specificity helps you maintain concentration by giving you a clear goal to work towards.

2. Measurable Goals: Tracking Progress and Celebrating Success.

Measuring progress is vital for staying motivated and assessing your financial journey. Measurable goals allow you to quantify your achievements and track how close you are to reaching your target. Consider using metrics such as dollar amounts, percentages, or specific milestones. For instance, "Increase my investment portfolio by 15% within one year" or "Reduce monthly expenses by 10% by the end of the quarter." Measuring your progress enables you to celebrate milestones and make adjustments when necessary.

3. Achievable Goals: Balancing Ambition and Realism.

Though having lofty aspirations is wonderful, it's crucial to establish practically reachable objectives. A realistic objective takes into account your time, knowledge, and financial resources. Evaluate your financial status and see if you can achieve your objective. While you should push yourself, don't forget to position yourself for success. For example, it might not be realistic to aim for a million-dollar investment in a year if your starting salary is tiny. Instead, concentrate on steady progress and modify your objectives as your situation changes.

4. Relevant Goals: Aligning with Your Financial Priorities

Relevance ensures that your goals align with your overall financial priorities and aspirations. Consider what matters most to you and how your goals contribute to those priorities. Are you focused on early retirement, funding your children's education, or starting a business? By setting relevant goals, you ensure that your efforts are directed towards what truly matters to you. For example, if you prioritize financial independence, your goals might revolve around building a robust investment portfolio or creating multiple income streams.

5. Time-Bound Goals: Adding a Sense of Urgency

Time-bound objectives force you to be accountable and give you a sense of urgency. You can make a schedule for accomplishing your goals by establishing a deadline. This fosters regular action and discourages procrastination. Think about giving your goals deadlines that are short-, medium-, and long-term. Like "Pay off credit card debt within six months" rather than "Achieve a net worth of $500,000 in five years." Time-bound objectives provide you with a precise deadline so you can track your progress and make any required modifications as you go.

CHAPTER 4

The Hidden Costs of Debt: Managing and Minimizing Debt

When used wisely, debt can help you reach your financial objectives—like buying a house or paying for schooling. But it's crucial to understand the unstated expenses of debt and to effectively manage and reduce it.

However, what is the hidden cost of debt?

Hidden debt describes debt that is not clearly or openly recorded in financial statements or other papers available to the public, making it challenging for stakeholders to determine the actual financial standing of an organization.

Aspiring businesswoman Sarah wants to open her own specialty clothes store. She chooses to get a bank business loan to finance her company's endeavor. Even if the loan gives her the money she needs to open her store, there are unstated expenses related to the debt.

Hidden costs

Interest Expenses: The business loan comes with an interest rate, which means Sarah will have to make regular interest payments on top of repaying the principal amount borrowed. The interest expenses can add up significantly over the loan's duration and increase the overall cost of borrowing.

Loan Origination Fees: When Sarah obtains the business loan, she may be required to pay loan origination fees. These fees cover the administrative costs associated with processing the loan application and can represent a notable upfront expense.

Prepayment Penalties: Some business loans come with prepayment penalties, which are charges imposed if Sarah decides to repay the loan before the agreed-upon term. These penalties can discourage early repayment and limit Sarah's flexibility in managing her debt.

Opportunity Cost: By taking on debt, Sarah may be using funds that could have been invested in other aspects of her business. This opportunity cost represents the potential benefits or returns that Sarah could have gained if she had used the funds differently, such as investing in marketing, expanding inventory, or improving the store's infrastructure.

What makes a debt good or bad?

Generally speaking, good debt is borrowing that is utilized to fund assets or investments that have the potential to appreciate or produce income over time.

Let's check out this scenario;

Good Debt - Mortgage Loan

Sarah and Mark are a young couple who decide to buy their first home. They take out a mortgage loan to finance the purchase. The home they buy is in a desirable location and has the potential for appreciation over time. They make regular mortgage payments, which include both interest and principal and gradually build equity in their property. As the years go by, the value of their home increases, and they benefit from both the pride of homeownership and the potential financial gains. In this scenario, the mortgage loan is considered good debt because it enables Sarah and Mark to acquire an asset that appreciates and provides long-term stability and potential wealth accumulation.

Bad debt

Bad debt generally refers to borrowing used for non-essential purchases or items that do not generate long-term value or income.

Bad Debt - High-Interest Consumer Loan for Vacation.

Louisa and Charles are a couple who decide to take a luxurious vacation to an exotic destination. Instead of saving up for the trip, they opt to take out a high-interest consumer loan to cover the expenses. After returning from the vacation, they find themselves burdened with debt and struggling to make the high monthly payments. The memories of the vacation fade quickly, but the debt remains, causing financial stress and limiting their ability to achieve other financial goals. In this scenario, the consumer loan for a non-essential expense like a vacation is considered a bad debt due to its high interest rates, lack of long-term value, and negative impact on Louisa and Charles's financial well-being.

Now let's explore the differences between the two couples' debt.

Louisa and Charles

Bad Debt (High-Interest Consumer Loan for Vacation):

Purpose: The loan is taken out to finance a non-essential expense, namely a luxurious vacation.

Interest Rates: The loan carries high-interest rates, which means that Sarah and John will end up paying a significant amount of interest over time.

Value: The vacation itself does not provide long-term value or appreciating assets. The memories fade quickly, leaving them with only the burden of debt.

Financial Impact: The high monthly payments associated with the loan strain Louisa and Charles's finances, making it difficult for them to meet other financial goals or save for the future. It causes financial stress and limits their financial flexibility.

Sarah and Mark

Good Debt (Mortgage Loan)

Purpose: The loan is taken out to finance the purchase of a home, which is considered an essential and appreciating asset.

Interest Rates: Mortgage loans generally have lower interest rates compared to consumer loans, making them more affordable in the long run.

Value: The home purchased with the mortgage loan has the potential for appreciation over time. As the property value increases, Sarah and Mark build equity and potentially gain long-term wealth.

Financial Impact: While mortgage payments are a regular financial commitment, they are typically manageable and can be considered an investment in the future. Homeownership provides stability and the potential for financial gains, such as selling the property at a higher value or using it for rental income.

CHAPTER 5

The money mindset: Exploring the beliefs and attitudes towards money.

Our beliefs are the lens through which we view the

world, including our perspective on money.

Our beliefs and attitudes towards money play a significant role in shaping our financial journey. Whether we realize it or not, our mindset surrounding money can have a profound impact on our financial decisions, habits, and overall financial well-being. Money is a tool that is very vital in our lives which helps to make life easier in all facets of our lives. A lot of people unknowingly carry limiting beliefs about money which is hindering their financial growth *"Money is the root of all evil" or " I will never be wealthy"*

1 Timothy 6:10 <u>For the love of money</u> is a root of all kinds of evil. Some people, eager for money, have wandered from the faith and pierced themselves with many griefs.

About the underlined sentence, **the love of money** refers to an unhealthy and obsessive desire for wealth, where money becomes the driving force behind one's actions, choices, and decisions. When individuals prioritize money above all else, it can lead to moral compromises, strained relationships, and a loss of connection to one's values and beliefs.

Meaning money in the actual sense is not evil but rather, the love of it makes it evil. This notion and misconception has made a lot of people particularly Christians poor by the beliefs they have about money making them exhibit unpleasant attitudes towards it.

A vital first step towards financial empowerment is understanding our money perspective. We can recognize any limiting beliefs, change our viewpoints, and develop a more positive connection with money by investigating our attitudes and beliefs surrounding it. Remember, change begins with awareness, and by embarking on this journey of self-reflection and growth, we can reshape our financial future.

CHAPTER 6

The Illusion of Easy Money: Debunking Common Myths

We are inundated with messages about easy money and rapid prosperity in today's fast-paced world. It seems sense that many people fall victim to the delusion of easy money given the prevalence of get-rich-quick scams and instant success stories. But we will dispel some popular misconceptions about quick money in this chapter and explain the truth about it.

Myth 1: It is easy to make money

The idea that making money doesn't require hard work or effort is one of the most pervasive fallacies. While it's true that some people may find unanticipated riches, the truth is that sustained prosperity necessitates commitment, tenacity, and a readiness to make the required efforts.

Myth 2: There is a magic recipe to get rich overnight

The notion that there is a magic formula or a quick route to quick wealth is another seductive illusion. The truth is that these types of shortcuts, whether in the form of secret investment strategies or "safe" trading opportunities, are rare. It takes time, patience, and a firm understanding of financial concepts to make money.

Myth 3: Success comes without risks

Many people believe that success and financial gain come without risks. They envision a scenario where they can make money without taking any chances or facing any setbacks. However, every successful person knows that risk is an inherent part of any worthwhile endeavor. It's important to calculate risks, make informed decisions, and be prepared to face challenges along the way.

Myth 4: All issues can be solved by money

One widespread misperception is that money can solve every issue. Money by itself cannot provide happiness, fulfillment, or true success, even while having enough money can undoubtedly reduce some stress. Relationships, self-improvement, and a feeling of purpose are just a few of the areas that true prosperity embraces.

Myth5: It is possible to make easy money

Jeremiah 17:11

"Like a partridge that hatches eggs it did not lay are those who gain riches by unjust means. When their lives are half gone, their riches will desert them, and in the end, they will prove to be fools."

Last but not least, some people think that easy money can last forever. However, experience has shown that there are frequently even faster losses to coincide with swift profits. Easy money leads to a series of destruction due to the illicit means of gaining it.

Laying a strong foundation, making thoughtful plans, and concentrating on adding value for others are all necessary to build lasting prosperity. Durable wealth develops gradually, whereas easy money frequently disappears.

The illusion of easy money can be enticing, but it's crucial to approach it with a critical mindset by debunking common myths surrounding easy money, so we can develop a realistic comprehension of what it takes to achieve financial success.

CONCLUSION

We are reminded that although spending may seem appealing, true financial independence comes from learning how to earn and manage money sensibly. The book equips readers to embrace mindful spending, break free from the cycle of quick gratification, and set out on a path toward long-term success with actionable ideas and a splash of inspiration. As this enlightening tale draws to an end, keep in mind that although earning money might be challenging, with the correct attitude, spending can be used as a tactical instrument to achieve financial success. Remember this.

ACKNOWLEDGEMENT

My Sincere Gratitude to Dennis Dornyo, Ebenezer Kofi Owusu (A.K.A Coach Eben), Pastor Lawrence Boafo, and my siblings.

BOOKS BY THIS AUTHOR

Unveiling A New Dawn

Transition In Human Life

The Psychology Of Spending